Famous Women in History
STAGECOACH MARY
FEARLESS OLD WEST MAIL CARRIER

WAYNE L. WILSON

© 2025 by Curious Fox Books™, an imprint of Fox Chapel Publishing Company, Inc.

Famous Women in History: Stagecoach Mary is a revision of *Wonder Women: Heroines of History: Stagecoach Mary*, published in 2019 by Purple Toad Publishing, Inc. Reproduction of its contents is strictly prohibited without written permission from the rights holder.

Paperback ISBN 979-8-89094-154-1
Hardcover ISBN 979-8-89094-155-8

Library of Congress Control Number: 2024946988

To learn more about the other great books from Fox Chapel Publishing, or to find a retailer near you, call toll-free 800-457-9112, send mail to , 903 Square Street, Mount Joy, PA 17552, or visit us at *www.FoxChapelPublishing.com*.

We are always looking for talented authors. To submit an idea, please send a brief inquiry to acquisitions@foxchapelpublishing.com.

Fox Chapel Publishing makes every effort to use environmentally friendly paper for printing.

Printed in China

Chapter One
Danger in the Pass 4
Mail Carrier John W. Curry 11

Chapter Two
Slavery, Friendship, and Freedom 12
The Ursuline Nuns at St. Peter's Mission 17

Chapter Three
A New Life in Montana 18
Buckboard Wagons 23

Chapter Four
An Amazing Worker 24
Saloons of the Old West 31

Chapter Five
A Woman of Letters 32
Mail Carrier Polly Martin 39
Timeline 40
Chapter Notes 42
Further Reading 44
Books 44
Works Consulted 44
On the Internet 45
Glossary 46
Index 48

DANGER IN THE PASS

CHAPTER ONE

"What's wrong with you tonight, Moses?" Mary asked her mule as they trudged through a snow-covered mountain pass. "You're moving about as fast as a snail."

Moses, who was ahead of the two horses pulling the wagon, lifted his head and snorted.

"That wasn't very nice," she said. "We've got to get all this freight and food to the mission as soon as we can. The nuns and schoolchildren are waiting on us. You know this route as well as me. I need you to move faster so the horses will follow your lead."

Moses bobbed his head but didn't go any faster.

"Are you still mad at me, Moses? Well, I declare, your temper is as bad as mine sometimes. I didn't have a choice. I was forced to leave you and the horses two nights ago. That snowstorm made it too difficult to see. And the snow was too deep for you to travel in. You would have gotten stuck. At least the

Stagecoach Mary often used a freight wagon to haul her stock. This heavy four-wheeled vehicle was often pulled by pack animals such as horses, mules, or oxen. It was used to haul goods, farming equipment, food supplies, and sometimes people.

CHAPTER ONE

Before horses were brought to North America, Native Americans, commonly wore snowshoes to hunt bison. Snowshoes were necessary in places where snow fell deep and often.

trees protected you from the weather when I tied you three up. I'm the one who should be angry. I put on snowshoes and carried all those sacks of mail on my shoulders for ten miles in the freezing snow! Oh well, at least tonight we got a little light on the road from the full moon."

Moses's ears flapped, but he wouldn't look at her.
"Look . . . it's my job to deliver the mail. I haven't missed a day yet, and I don't plan to! I'm the first black woman mail carrier in not only Montana, but the whole country! So I've got a lot to prove. The post office thinks women are too soft and scared to deliver mail on these dangerous roads. But not Mary Fields! I showed them that even though I'm in my sixties, I can hitch a team of six horses faster than anybody. They call me Stagecoach Mary! And I'm not afraid of anything—not even bad weather or robbers!"

DANGER IN THE PASS

Moses looked around nervously. He stared for a long time at the trees along the path. Suddenly, he stopped. He stomped his hooves and brayed. His loud hee-haws echoed in the chilly air. The horses looked confused as they shifted back and forth in their harnesses. They started neighing, and Mary could see their breath.

"What's wrong with everybody? You see something, Moses?"

Shadows raced across their path, snarling and growling.

Wolves!

Moses and the frightened horses bucked and reared as the wolves attacked. The wagon jerked and then dumped the supplies and Mary into the freezing snow. She pulled her .38 Smith and Wesson from her belt and fired it into the air. Luckily, the loud shots made the wolf pack

Hungry wolves often hung around frontiersmen, explorers, fur traders, soldiers, and missionaries' camps. Occasionally, they attacked a party's horses and mules, especially if the animal strayed or was left alone.

CHAPTER ONE

flee into the forest, but Mary knew they weren't gone. They desperately wanted the food.

"Well, fellas, it looks like it's going to be a long night. It's too dark to repair the wagon, so we're going to have to wait until morning. But don't you worry! Stagecoach Mary is going to protect you from those hungry wolves!"

She patted Moses on the head and fed him and the horses some carrots and sugar to calm them down.

"Now I get it. So that's what was wrong, huh, Moses? I'm so sorry. You knew those wolves were following us, didn't you?" She felt his icy whiskers as he crushed his face affectionately against hers.

Mary grabbed her rifle and sat on top of a large crate with her pistol in her lap. She pulled out one of her homemade cigars and lit it.

"Okay, wolves, make your move. I'm ready for you!" She shouted as she cocked her rifle.

The wolves made a few more attempts throughout the night, but Mary was able to

How to recognize a gray wolf

GRAY WOLF
- Color: light gray to black
- Dimensions: 2.5 feet tall, 5-6 feet long
- Broad snout
- Round ears
- 80-120 pounds
- Paw size: 4" x 5"

COYOTE
- Color: light gray/brown
- Dimensions: 1.5 feet tall, 4 feet long
- Tall pointed ears
- Narrow snout
- 20-50 pounds
- Paw size: 2" x 2.5"

Wolves are protected by federal law under the Endangered Species Act.
Source: U.S. Fish and Wildlife Service

Mary knew the difference between the coyote and the gray wolf, which was more common in Montana. Coyotes were also called prairie jackals or brush wolves. Gray wolves were also called big prairie wolves or loafers. The wolves would often rest, or loaf around, after eating a big meal.

keep them at bay. Every time she heard footsteps in the snow or saw the horses get nervous, she'd fire the rifle or pistol into the air. The moonlight helped because it would reflect off the wolves' yellow eyes as they crouched in the snow. By dawn, they were completely gone except for their footprints.

Mary was a big, strong woman, so she was able to right the wagon, repair the wheels, and reload the supplies. When she arrived at the mission, she had never seen so many smiling faces. The girls greeted her with big hugs as soon as she stepped down from the wagon. Her closest friend, Mother Amadeus, also welcomed her with a warm hug.

"Mary, we were so worried about you when you didn't show up. Are you okay?"

Pioneers heading west were responsible for the maintenance and repairs of their vehicles. The best-prepared travelers carried some tools and knew how to fix wagon wheels. Their lives depended on keeping the wagon in the best condition possible.

CHAPTER ONE

Ursuline nuns and Native American students line up in front of St. Peter's Mission near Cascade, Montana. "Stagecoach" Mary Fields sits in a wagon at the right.

"Of course I am, Sister. You know better than that! Nothing can stop Stagecoach Mary from bringing you the supplies you need. But I don't have time to talk. Let me get these things off the wagon so these children can eat!"

Mary acted tough, but it really made her feel good to have so many people happy to see her.

MAIL CARRIER JOHN W. CURRY

John W. Curry is one of the earliest known African American letter carriers. He started out as a clerk in the Washington, D.C., post office in 1867. He worked for the postal service for the next thirty-two years. On April 20, 1870, he joined the carrier force.

Curry was an active member of the National Association of Letter Carriers (NALC). When he passed away in 1899, the NALC wrote about his "steadfast devotion to duty" and his concern for the rights of letter carriers.[1] Curry took part in many political causes and was praised for playing a large role in opening the door for black letter carriers.

The 1905 National Association of Letter Carriers at their first Biennial Convention.

SLAVERY, FRIENDSHIP, AND
FREEDOM

CHAPTER TWO

Most historians believe Mary was born into slavery around 1832 in Tennessee. Some believe she was born in Arkansas. Since Mary did not know the exact day she was born, she celebrated two birthdays a year.[1] Many slaves did not know when they were born. Slaves were treated like property. They were counted and listed in the record books, but not always by name.

Very little is known about Mary's family. It has been said that her mother was a house slave and her father, Buck, worked in the fields.[2] Buck was sold after Mary was born. Her mother, Susanna, wanted Mary to have a last name. Since Buck worked in the fields, she decided it would be Fields. Susanna died when Mary was fourteen.

Mary outgrew the boys her age. She was ordered to work in the cotton fields doing heavy labor with the boys and men. Working and competing with males all the time may be part of the reason Mary became so fearless and independent. By the time she

Dolly Johnson, a house slave, holds the grandson of Tennessee State Senator Andrew Johnson. Johnson also served as President of the United States. House slaves lived in the house of the slave owner. They cooked, cleaned, and cared for the children.

CHAPTER TWO

Because Mary was larger and stronger, she often did heavy labor in the fields (usually a task given to men and boys). The sacks of cotton were heavy—weighing 60 to 70 pounds.

was 18, she was already six feet tall and weighed over 200 pounds.

Around this time, Mary met a young woman named Sarah Dunne. Some claim that Mary was owned by the Warner family in Arkansas. She met Sarah because one of the daughters of the family married a Dunne. Others say that Mary and Sarah met because Mary was a servant of Judge Edmond Dunne, Sarah's oldest brother.

Sarah became Mary's lifelong friend and had a major impact on her life. The two were very close, yet very different. As one historian wrote:

Sarah Dunne had a fair complexion and blond hair and blue eyes and was descended from a wealthy Irish family. Mary was dark skinned with black hair and dark eyes, the child of slave parents. Sarah was frail and delicate. Mary was strong and sturdy. Sarah was educated early in life. Mary became literate only years later. Sarah was refined and patient; Mary was rough and quick tempered.[3]

In 1865, Congress passed the 13th Amendment, which formally freed the slaves in the United States. Fields was 33. She found work as a chambermaid on the *Robert E. Lee*, a Mississippi River steamboat. She loved talking about how she took part in the famous steamboat race in 1870, when the *Robert E. Lee* beat the steamboat *Natchez* in a three-day

14

SLAVERY, FRIENDSHIP, AND FREEDOM

race from New Orleans to St. Louis.

Mary again met Sarah Dunne's brother, Judge Dunne, on that steamship. Soon, she was hired as a servant of the judge and his wife. Mary learned from the judge that Sarah Dunne was now a nun living at the Ursuline Catholic convent in Toledo, Ohio.

One day, Mary decided to travel to Ohio to visit the Ursuline Convent of the Sacred Heart. Some say it was to see Sarah and to find work there. Others say that after Judge Dunne's wife, Josephine, died in 1883, Fields was asked to take the family's five children to live with their aunt. By this time, Sarah was Mother Mary Amadeus, the Mother Superior of the convent.

The *Robert E. Lee* steamboat, built in Indiana in 1866, was named after the commander of the Confederate Army. In a famous 1870 steamboat race, it beat the *Natchez*, the former speed record holder.

The sisters agreed to take Mary in. Mother Amadeus helped her friend get settled in her new room there. When she asked Mary if she wanted anything else, Mary replied: "Yes, a good cigar and a drink."[4]

Mother Amadeus gave Mary a room on the first floor of the convent. The sisters called her "Black Mary." She lived up to the nickname. Mary liked dressing in all black. She'd wear a black apron over her black dress (or sometimes black pants) and put on a black skullcap. She also loved smoking black cigars.[5]

Mary was a hard worker. She washed the laundry, bought supplies, and cooked in the convent's kitchen. She was paid $50 per year. At times, she battled with the nuns over her wages when she wasn't paid on time. Mary was not afraid to express her feelings. This shocked many

CHAPTER TWO

An 1892 photo of the Ursuline Convent and Girls' School at St. Peter's Mission. The chapel with the bell tower was the sleeping area for the priest. The lower structure housed the kitchen and the area where the nuns slept.

white people. They expected people of color to never complain and always be obedient.

Mary had a hard time adjusting to the quiet and sheltered life of the convent. She liked to talk tough and drink whiskey. The nuns often complained about her temper and "difficult" nature.[6]

Mary planted crops and took care of the convent's garden and courtyard. She watched the schoolchildren like a hawk to make sure no one messed up her well-kept lawn. Sister Mary Grace Connelly, a former Ursuline archivist who had heard many personal accounts of life with Mary, said in a 1981 interview, "God help anyone who walked on the lawn after Mary had cut it!"[7]

Mary loved to relax with her pet dog and play her banjo and harmonica. She also enjoyed talking politics. On Election Day, she'd hitch a ride to town, smoking her black cigar, to support her favorite candidate.[8]

THE URSULINE NUNS AT ST. PETER'S MISSION

St. Peter's Mission was founded in the 1860s by a Catholic religious order called the Jesuits. It was a stone structure that served as a school for white and Native American boys. Father DeSmet baptized the first Blackfeet in the area.

Mother Amadeus Dunne and the Ursuline nuns arrived there in 1884 to help the priests start a girls' school. When the Jesuits left the mission, the nuns had very little money and struggled to survive. In the early 1900s, two fires destroyed many of the buildings. The schools were closed, and the mission was abandoned. The only building remaining today is a small, white wood-frame church.

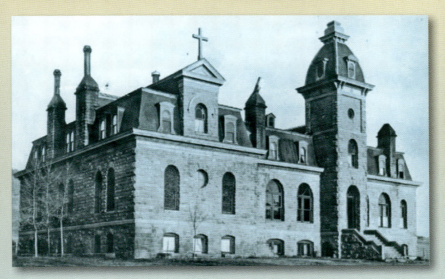

The Ursuline Convent and Girls' School at St. Peter's Mission in 1892

A NEW LIFE IN MONTANA

CHAPTER THREE

Mary grew very close to Mother Amadeus Dunne. It saddened her when she learned that the Mother Superior was leaving to do missionary work in Montana. The Jesuits had asked the Ursuline sisters to help them build mission schools for both white pioneer and Native American children.

In 1884, Mother Amadeus led five nuns on a 1,600-mile journey west through the dangerous wilds of the Montana Territory. They wanted to build missions on the Cheyenne, Crow, Blackfoot, and Gros Ventre-Assiniboine Reservation in central and eastern Montana.[1] The sisters were not ready for the harsh winters, when temperatures dropped to forty degrees below zero.

However, in 1884, Mother Amadeus founded an Ursuline convent in Central Montana. She also helped the Jesuit priests open a school for Blackfoot girls. But the terrible living conditions—sleeping on cold, wet cabin floors, barely eating, and working too hard with little sleep—affected her health. She became ill

Montana is one of the most beautiful places in the world. But in the 19th century, the fierce winter storms and the rough terrain made it a difficult place to live.

CHAPTER THREE

Mary didn't hesitate to embark on a long and sometimes dangerous journey to help her longtime friend Mother Amadeus.

with pneumonia while setting up St. Peter's Mission schools.[2]

When Mary heard that Mother Amadeus was deathly ill, she swiftly packed her bag. Nothing was going to stop the fifty-three-year-old Fields from helping her dear friend. In March 1885, Mary, Mother Stanislaus, Sister Saint Rose, and Sister Mary of the Angels rode the Northern Pacific Railroad across seven states to Helena, Montana.

They most likely traveled the next 70 miles to St. Peter's Mission by stagecoach. The rest of the way they rode through the snow in a buckboard, a wagon with four large wheels drawn by a horse. The buckboard would get them through the rougher terrain of mountains, hills, and forest.

When the rescue party arrived, they were stunned to see the Ursuline settlement. There, in the icy snow-swept area, were two beat-up cabins. The women rushed inside one and were relieved to find Mother Mary Amadeus still alive, but lying on the bitterly cold dirt floor.[3]

Mary helped nurse Mother Amadeus back to health. Even though Mother Amadeus was a great leader, Mary felt she couldn't do it alone in such a rough environment. Mary was a survivor and knew how to get food and shelter for the sisters when necessary. She was willing to deal with the freezing cold, rainy winters, and living in log cabins—as long as she could be there to help her beloved friend. She insisted on

A NEW LIFE IN MONTANA

staying at St. Peter's Mission, and Montana became her new home.

Mary learned from the nuns the type of work they were expected to do. She baked bread with them; she also washed, ironed, and mended all the clothes of the Jesuit household. She and the nuns did these tasks with little food and poor lodging. They huddled in a box in a wagon throughout the winter months and their many blizzards. They often suffered from frostbite, but they relied on their faith to keep pushing forward.[4]

Mary was very close with the nuns. She supported their work by helping them in many ways, including the building of a stone convent.

One of the two cabins built by the Jesuits decades before served as the white girls' school and dormitory. These students began attending classes on November 10, 1884, eleven days after the nuns arrived. Miners passing through the area built a single-room log cabin for the sisters. The nuns lived there for a short time before establishing it as a Native American boarding school.

On March 7, 1885, eleven female students arrived from the Blackfoot reservation. They called the nuns, who wore layers of black clothing, "Black Robes."[5]

The nuns were able to get a small woodstove. Finally, they could sleep in warmth at night. After school hours, the nuns used the space for work duties. At night they slept on the floor. When dawn came, they attended mass and went back to their duties.

Mary helped in ways the sisters never could. She used her strength and plantation know-how to help develop the mission. She picked out

CHAPTER THREE

The nuns (from left to right) Mother Mary Amadeus Dunne, Sister Saint Ignatius, and Sister Saint Thomas with Native American students at St. Peter's Mission. Even though the sisters sincerely wanted to educate the students, these types of boarding schools were damaging to the children in the long run and destructive of their cultures.

a section of land that was perfect for planting a vegetable garden. Because she was an expert on farming, Mary was able to feed the nuns and the growing population of students. Among the Blackfeet she was known as the "White Crow." The Native Americans said, "She behaved like a white woman but had black skin."[6] No one in that region had seen or met anyone like Mary Fields. In 1885, Mary was the first African American woman to step foot in the small town of Cascade, Montana. This was the beginning of more "firsts" to come.

BUCKBOARD WAGONS

Horace and James Buck created the buckboard wagon around 1841. They went to Europe to study wagon making and then came back home to Portland, Oregon, to start a carriage business.

The buckboard was simple and light. It had four large wheels and a wide seat. Springy wooden slats extended from the front to the rear axle. The seat was attached to the boards, which made the ride less bumpy. Iron rails three to four inches high around the back of the wagon held in supplies or packages. In front, a separate board acted as both a footrest and protection for the driver from the horses' hooves in case they bucked. The board gave the "buckboard" wagon its name. Farmers, ranchers, and cowboys used these wagon to carry supplies.

A buckboard wagon

AN AMAZING WORKER

CHAPTER FOUR

"[Mary Fields] did everything that we couldn't."[1]
–Nun's entry from the St. Peter's Ursuline Annals

Mary Fields was a skilled horsewoman. She regularly drove the mission horses from aboard a buckboard, buggy, or farm wagon. Driving horses on such rough roads required knowledge, skill, strength, and courage. If a vehicle broke down in a remote area, it was up to the driver to repair it. The mission was 34 miles from the closest outpost. The town of Cascade was 19 miles away.

Mary hauled lumber, stone, tools, medicine, hardware, dry goods, and food in the wagon. Besides tending her garden, she also hunted wild game and built a henhouse. By 1887, she was tending more than 400 hens and ducks, which provided meat and eggs for the congregation.[2]

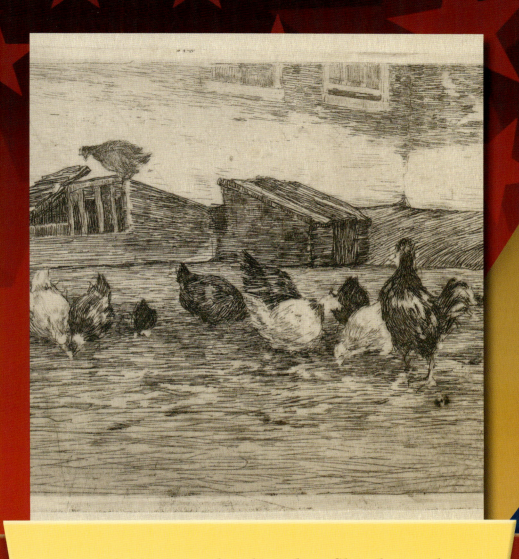

Mary Fields was a hard worker. She chopped wood, dug latrines, maintained large gardens, and built a schoolhouse and chapel. She also built a chicken coop for her livestock, probably similar to the style illustrated here.

CHAPTER FOUR

Mary was always armed with a rifle and at least one pistol. She was skilled with her 1876 Winchester carbine shown here, but could effectively use most firearms.

Mary was an expert with firearms. She owned an 1876 Winchester carbine, a huge rifle. As legend has it, she "couldn't miss a thing within fifty paces."[3] When Mary drove the mission buckboard, she kept a rifle by her side and carried a .38 Smith & Wesson pistol under her apron for protection. She did not hesitate to pull out her pistol if someone tried to steal her cargo.

The army chaplain at Fort Keough, Father Eli Landesmith, really liked Mary when he met her in 1887. Mary told him about how she had to kill a skunk after it broke into her coop and killed 62 of the chicks. The chaplain recorded their talk in his diary: "I asked her the following question: Mary, did not the pole cat [skunk] throw his stench all over you? Her answer was 'Oh, no Father. I attacked and killed him from the front, not the rear!"[4]

AN AMAZING WORKER

Chicken coops are vulnerable to predators like skunks. Mary kept her sense of humor while dedicating herself to protecting the chicks.

The nuns often said they didn't know what they would have done without Mary's help. She took on tasks such as housekeeping, gardening, laundry, painting, and building maintenance. Mary devotedly worked at the convent for 10 years, from 1885 to 1895. She accepted room and board but refused to be paid.[5] The mission was her home, and she thought she was going to be there for the rest of her life. She knew the convent was struggling to make money, and she wanted to help in any way she could. When she needed money for herself, she sometimes worked freight jobs.

CHAPTER FOUR

Mary's buckskin dresses were a different style from the dresses worn in 1913 by these Kiowa girls, but the buckskin was tanned using the same methods developed by Native American tribes.

Mary liked to dress in men's frontier clothing. According to researchers Henry Gates and Julie Wolf, she usually wore "a buckskin dress over buckskin pants (made from hide she'd learn to tan herself), topped by a buffalo coat and a black hat."[6] Still, even though Cascade residents gossiped about her wearing men's clothes, Fields was often seen in photographs wearing women's clothing, too. In photos showing her driving a wagon, walking to town, gardening, or posing with the Cascade baseball team, she is seen wearing long skirts, wool or cotton dresses, and the aprons that rural western women wore during that era. During the winters she wore a man's wool overcoat, because the women's overcoats were too small for her frame.[7]

AN AMAZING WORKER

Mary decided to celebrate her unknown birthday each year on March 15. In March, the nuns showed their love for her by having a birthday celebration at St. Peter's Mission. The mission students would give her a cake, presents, and a birthday cheer.[8]

Mary enjoyed being around young people, and her students loved her. During one May Day event, she led the young women on a trip through meadows and hills, where they had a picnic. Later, they

A group of nuns and novitiates (nuns in training) stand in front of the St. Peter's Mission chapel and nuns' residence in 1897.

CHAPTER FOUR

gathered wildflowers, which they bundled into May Day posies. They gave the flowers to St. Peter's parishioners.

In 1890, the Native American boarders had grown to 113 girls. Mary was a strong mother figure for them.[9] Because she was neither a nun nor white, the students felt they could talk with her about their problems.

Mary was sure that St. Peter's would be her final home. But, once again, her temper got her into trouble.

Mother Amadeus with a Blackfoot girl. Although she could be a comforting presence for these girls, many of them related more with Mary Fields, a former slave.

SALOONS OF THE OLD WEST

When the pioneers began exploring and moving into the Wild West, saloons popped up wherever they settled. The first western saloons were tents where travelers, cowboys, miners, and soldiers could stop for food and drink. As populations increased, saloons became more popular. For example, in 1883, Livingston, Montana, had only 3,000 residents, but 33 saloons![10]

In those rough days, the whiskey served to customers was pretty horrible. It was made with raw alcohol, burnt sugar, and chewing tobacco. It was given names like Fire Water, Redeye, Bug Juice, Bottled Courage, Dynamite, Coffin Varnish, Tarantula Juice, Taos Lightning, and Gut Warmer.

Most saloons had poker tables for cowboys, railroad workers, prospectors, lawmen, soldiers, miners, and cowboys trying to make a fortune. Professional gamblers like Doc Holliday and Wild Bill Hickok sometimes tested their six-shooter skills on cheaters. Mining camps such as Deadwood, Leadville, and Tombstone were known for their gunfights over card games. In some of the more crowded places, saloons didn't have front doors because these businesses never closed.[11]

Montana saloon, 1880

A WOMAN OF LETTERS

CHAPTER FIVE

The sisters adored and admired Mary. She had done a fantastic job building St. Peter's Mission. But they worried about her. She had a very bad temper. They invited her to join them in the Catholic services, but Mary liked hanging out with the men working around the convent. She drank liquor with them, talked tough, smoked cigars, argued, and won fistfights and shooting contests.

Mary played a major role in building the sisterhood a convent, three stone buildings, and a church. She did most of the hard labor herself, hauling stone and lumber on her back from the wagon to the site. She would not accept any help from men. When it was time for the sisters to move from the log cabins to their new stone building, Mary hauled Mother Amadeus's belongings in a wheelbarrow to the new site.[1]

As the only black woman in the area, Mary was often called terrible names. The nuns told her to ignore the name-calling, but she couldn't do it. Her

A legend of the American West, Mary Fields was always well armed. Here she holds her giant of a rifle, and she was often seen with a pair of six-shooters strapped to her waist. She was six feet tall, tough, and had a fiery temper, but she was admired by many and fiercely loyal to the people she loved.

CHAPTER FIVE

Customers of the Old West saloons were usually all men looking for entertainment. Fist or even gunfights often broke out over card games if the players were drinking too much.

explosive temper got her into fights. An angry worker challenged Mary to a battle because she made $2 a month more than him. It turned into a shoot-out. The fight ended when one of her bullets hit him in his backside. Another time, Mary got mad at a man who yelled insults at her. She threw stones at him until he ran away crying for help.

A white schoolgirl wrote an essay about Mary. She said the woman "drinks whiskey, and she swears, and she is a republican, which makes her a low, foul creature."[2] A local paper wrote that Mary "broke more noses than any other person in central Montana and that any man that challenged her was a hard-headed fool." Some called her the "Terror of the Countryside."[3]

Many people outside the convent did not see the kind, loyal Mary with the heart of gold. Sister McBride said in a book about the mission that Mary "was at times troublesome, but her unfailing loyalty endeared her to the nuns and children."[4]

Complaints about Mary were sent to Montana's Bishop Brondel. He ordered the sisters "to send that black woman away!"[5] The nuns were

A WOMAN OF LETTERS

upset, but they had to obey him. After ten years of devoted service, a brokenhearted Mary packed her bags and left.

Mother Amadeus showed her love and appreciation by setting her up in the restaurant business. Mary, by this time in her early sixties, started a new career. But Mary was too kind and generous. She kept giving away meals for free, especially to the poor. She just couldn't refuse food to anyone who was hungry. Both of her restaurants failed.[6]

Mother Amadeus later found the perfect job for her struggling friend—as a U.S. Postal Service worker. However, the postal service felt the job was too physically demanding for women because of the travel, and too dangerous because of bandits. Women, reports the postal service, were considered "delicate and fragile."[7]

Not Mary Fields.

Out of all the applicants, Mary was the fastest to hitch a team of six horses, even against men half her age. She became the second female and the first African-American woman star route mail carrier in United States history.

Mary's 19-mile route was between Cascade and St. Peter's Mission. She could now see Mother Amadeus and the nuns on a daily basis. Seated on her stagecoach, she usually wore dark clothing, a

Almost all postal workers, like this one on a railway car, were white men. That was finally starting to change.

35

CHAPTER FIVE

skullcap, and a man's overcoat as she'd ride into town and back. Historian Tricia Wagner describes her as having a "jug of whiskey by her foot, a pistol packed under her apron, and a shotgun by her side."[8] Mary drove the route

A six-horse team pulls a mail-type wagon.

An 1895 regulation mail wagon in San Francisco. These wagons transported mail between post offices, their stations, and large cities. They were later phased out for lighter and cheaper screen wagons.

A WOMAN OF LETTERS

This mail wagon is in a National Postal Museum exhibit that explores the 1845 establishment of the star route. At the time, these wagons were the most efficient means of delivering the mail.

with horses and a mule named Moses. Soon she was called "Stagecoach Mary."

For eight years, Mary never missed a day's work. She didn't care about the long hours, low pay, or bad weather. She always made her deliveries. If the snow was too deep for her horses or Moses, she'd strap on snowshoes, throw the sack over her shoulders, and walk for miles to her destination.

Mary was in her seventies when she retired from the postal service. She was a legend and Cascade's most respected and loved citizen. She opened a laundry service in her home, and people finally saw the goodness in her and gave her a lot of business. The Cascade hotel provided free meals to her for the rest of her life. In 1912, her home was destroyed by a fire. People jumped in to help. They donated time, labor, clothing, and supplies to rebuild it for her.

CHAPTER FIVE

The mayor gave her special permission to drink at the saloons during a time when women weren't allowed to be inside. On her birthday they closed the schools and celebrated with her. She was a huge fan of the baseball team and traveled with the players to games. She presented flowers to players on both sides.

Mary Fields, who never married, died at the age of 82 on December 5, 1914. Her funeral was the largest one in the town's history. She was laid to rest at the foot of the mountains that led to St. Peter's Mission. Famous actor Gary Cooper, who was born in Montana, fondly remembered meeting Mary when he was a boy. He spoke highly of her to *Ebony* magazine in 1959. He ended the interview by saying, "Mary lived to be one of the freest souls ever to draw a breath or a thirty-eight."[9]

Stagecoach Mary Fields with her trusty shotgun. She was the second woman and the first African American female star route carrier in the United States.

MAIL CARRIER POLLY MARTIN

During the 1800s, women were viewed as too delicate and frail to be mail carriers. Women looking for jobs as contract or "star" route carriers had to be able to protect the mail and defend themselves. The first known female on a star route was Polly Martin. She drove her mail wagon from around 1860 to 1876, between Attleboro and South Attleboro, Massachusetts. Along with the mail, she carried express packages, telegraph messages, and one to six passengers.

In an 1884 *Boston Daily Globe* article about Polly Martin, she was described as a "tall, muscular woman." She remarked that driving the mail wagon "was pretty tough sometimes, in the winter. . . . Many a time I . . . got out and dug the horse out of the drifts."[10] During her 16 years of service, she was attacked by robbers only once. One of the robbers stepped into the road and grabbed the horse's reins. She pounded him with her horsewhip and kept going. She stated, "He tackled the wrong customer that time."[11]

Mail service woman, 1917

TIMELINE

1832?   Mary Fields is born, probably in Tennessee or Arkansas.

1835   Texians and the Mexican Army fight for Texas in the Battle of the Alamo.

1836   Samuel Colt invents the revolver.

1838   The Cherokee and other Native American peoples are forced to march from their homelands in the southeastern United States to Oklahoma along the "Trail of Tears."

1846   Mary's mother dies. The Mexican-American War begins.

1849   Harriet Tubman escapes slavery and becomes a leader of the Underground Railroad. The California Gold Rush begins.

1850   The Fugitive Slave Act of 1850 is passed, taking away the civil and political rights of escaped slaves. It also calls for harsh penalties to those who harbor or fail to arrest runaway slaves.

1857   In the *Dred Scott* case, the U.S. Supreme Court rules that Congress does not have the right to ban slavery and that slaves are not citizens.

1860   The Pony Express is founded.

1861   The American Civil War begins.

1863   President Lincoln signs the Emancipation Proclamation, freeing the slaves.

1865   The Thirteenth Amendment to the United States Constitution is passed, outlawing slavery.

1868   The Fourteenth Amendment is passed. It declares that African Americans should not be denied equal protection or due process of law.

1869   The First Transcontinental Railroad is completed when the final spike is driven in Utah Territory. Mary Fields begins working as a maid on the *Robert E. Lee*.

1870   The Fifteenth Amendment gives black Americans the right to vote. The famous three-day steamboat race occurs between the *Robert E. Lee* and *Natchez*.

TIMELINE

1883   Mary moves in with her friend Mother Amadeus in Toledo, Ohio, to help care for her friend's five nieces and nephews.

1884   Mother Amadeus Dunne is sent to Montana Territory to establish a school for Blackfoot girls at St. Peter's Mission, west of Cascade.

1885   Mary goes to St. Peter's Mission to help Mother Amadeus. She is the first African American woman to step foot in Cascade, Montana.

1895   Mary Fields becomes a star route mail carrier.

1896   In *Plessy v. Ferguson*, the U.S. Supreme Court holds that racial segregation is constitutional. It opens the door for Jim Crow laws in the South. Montana becomes the 41st state.

1909   The National Association for the Advancement of Colored People is founded.

1912   Mary's home is destroyed by fire. Townspeople pitch in to help her rebuild.

1914   In Montana, women are given the right to vote in all but federal elections. Mary Fields dies at the age of 82 from liver failure.

Horses did not usually gallop when pulling a stagecoach. Stagecoaches weighed over a ton. If fully loaded with passengers and supplies, the horses could not maintain a gallop for more than a few hundred feet. Riders might see their luggage left behind if the stagecoach was running late. Getting the mail and freight through was a driver's priority.

CHAPTER NOTES

Chapter 1. Danger in the Pass
1. National Postal Museum, "The History and Experience of African Americans in America's Postal Service," https://postalmuseum.si.edu/research-article/the-history-and-experience-of-african-americans-in-america%E2%80%99s-postal-service

Chapter 2. Slavery, Friendship, and Freedom
1. JC Reindl, " 'Stagecoach Mary' Broke Barriers of Race, Gender," *The Blade*, February 8, 2010, https://www.toledoblade.com/local/2010/02/08/Stagecoach-Mary-broke-barriers-of-race-gender.html
2. "The Life and Legend of Mary Fields," *Montana Women's History*, April 8, 2014, https://montanawomenshistory.org/the-life-and-legend-of-mary-fields/
3. Tricia Martineau Wagner, *African American Women of the Old West* (Helena, Montana: Twodot, 2007), p. 14.
4. Reindl.
5. Wagner, p. 17.
6. Erin Blakemore, "Meet Stagecoach Mary, the Daring Black Pioneer Who Protected Wild West Stagecoaches," *History*, September 14, 2017, https://www.history.com/news/meet-stagecoach-mary-the-daring-black-pioneer-who-protected-wild-west-stagecoaches
7. Reindl.
8. Wagner, p. 18.

Chapter 3. A New Life in Montana
1. Bruce A. Glasrud and Michael N. Searles (eds.), *Black Cowboys in the American West: On the Range, on the Stage, behind the Badge* (Norman: University of Oklahoma Press, 2016), pp. 150–151.
2. Ibid.
3. Ibid.
4. Ibid.
5. Ibid.
6. Tijana Radeska, "Mary Fields—The First African-American Woman Employed as a Mail Carrier in the United States," *The Vintage News*, October 10, 2010, https://www.thevintagenews.com/2016/10/10/mary-fields-first-african-american-woman-employed-mail-carrier-united-states-2/

Chapter 4. An Amazing Worker
1. Bruce A. Glasrud and Michael N. Searles (eds.), *Black Cowboys in the American West: On the Range, on the Stage, behind the Badge* (Norman: University of Oklahoma Press, 2016), p. 152.

CHAPTER NOTES

2. George Everett, "Mary Fields: Female Pioneer in Montana," *HISTORYNET*, June 12, https://www.historynet.com/mary-fields-female-pioneer-in-montana/?f
3. Tricia Martineau Wagner, *African American Women of the Old West* (Helena, Montana: Twodot, 2007), p. 20.
4. Gayle C. Shirley, *More Than Petticoats: Remarkable Montana Women* (Kearney: Morris Book Publishing, 2011), p. 3.
5. Dee Garceau-Hagen (ed.), *Portraits of Women in the American West* (New York: Routledge Taylor & Francis Group, 2005.), pp. 112–113.
6. Henry Louis Gates Jr., Julie Wolf, "Cigar-Smoking, Gun-Toting Mary Fields Carried Montana's Mail," February 16, 2015, https://www.theroot.com/cigar-smoking-gun-toting-mary-fields-carried-montana-s-1790858815
7. Garceau-Hagen, pp. 122–123.
8. Glasrud and Searles, p. 153.
9. Ibid.
10. Kathy Weiser-Alexander, "Saloons of the American West," Legends of America, August 2017. https://www.legendsofamerica.com/we-saloons/
11. Ibid.

Chapter 5. A Woman of Letters
1. George Everett, "Mary Fields: Female Pioneer in Montana," *HISTORYNET*, June 12, 2016, https://www.historynet.com/mary-fields-female-pioneer-in-montana/?f
2. Gayle C. Shirley, *More Than Petticoats: Remarkable Montana Women* (Kearney: Morris Book Publishing, 2011), p. 4.
3. Zachary Crockett, "Mary Fields: Former Slave, Pioneer Woman, Certified Badass," *Priceonomics*, n.d., https://priceonomics.com/mary-fields-former-slave-pioneer-woman-certified/
4. Shirley, p. 4.
5. Kathy Warnes, *Women of Every Complexion and Complexity*, "Mary Fields, Stage Coach Mail Driver, Sharp Shooter, Faithful Friend," n.d., https://womenofeverycomplexionandcomplexity.weebly.com/mary-fields-stage-coach-mail-driver-sharp-shooter-faithful-friend.html
6. Tricia Martineau Wagner, *African American Women of the Old West* (Helena, Montana: Twodot, 2007), p. 21.
7. Crockett.
8. Wagner, p. 22.
9. Kathryn S. Gardiner, "Forgotten Foremothers: 'Stagecoach Mary' Fields," *League of Women Voters of Indiana*, February 14, 2020, https://www.lwvin.org/content.aspx?page_id=5&club_id=42001&item_id=57635
10. "Women Mail Carriers," USPS, June 2007, https://about.usps.com/who-we-are/postal-history/women-carriers.pdf
11. Ibid.

FURTHER READING

Books

Furbee, Mary Rodd. *Outrageous Women of the American Frontier*. Hoboken, NJ: Wiley Publishing, 2007.

Miller, Robert H. *Once Upon a Time in the Black West*, Amazon Digital Services, 2018.

Winter, Jonah. *Wild Women of the Wild West*. New York: Holiday House, 2011.

Works Consulted

Butler, Anne M. *Across God's Frontiers: Catholic Sisters in the American West*, 1850–1920. Chapel Hill: The University of North Carolina Press, 2012.

Erin Blakemore. "Meet Stagecoach Mary, the Daring Black Pioneer Who Protected Wild West Stagecoaches." History, September 14, 2017, https://www.history.com/news/meet-stagecoach-mary-the-daring-black-pioneer-who-protected-wild-west-stagecoaches

Everett, George, "Mary Fields: Female Pioneer in Montana." HISTORYNET, June 12, 2016, https://www.historynet.com/mary-fields-female-pioneer-in-montana/?f

Garceau-Hagen, Dee (ed.). *Portraits of Women in the American West*. New York: Routledge Taylor & Francis Group, 2005.

Gates, Henry Louis, Jr., Julie Wolf. "Cigar-Smoking, Gun-Toting Mary Fields Carried Montana's Mail." February 16, 2015, https://www.theroot.com/cigar-smoking-gun-toting-mary-fields-carried-montana-s-1790858815

Glasrud, Bruce A., and Michael N. Searles (eds.). *Black Cowboys in the American West: On the Range, on the Stage, behind the Badge*. Norman: University of Oklahoma Press, 2016.

Reindl, JC. "Stagecoach Mary Broke Barriers of Race, Gender." *The Blade*, February 8, 2010. https://www.toledoblade.com/local/2010/02/08/Stagecoach-Mary-broke-barriers-of-race-gender.html

FURTHER READING

Warnes, Kathy. "Mary Fields, Stage Coach Mail Driver, Sharp Shooter, Faithful Friend." n.d., https://womenofeverycomplexionandcomplexity.weebly.com/mary-fields-stage-coach-mail-driver-sharp-shooter-faithful-friend.html

McConnell, Miantae Metcalf. *Deliverance. Mary Fields: First African American Woman Star Route Mail Carrier in the United States—A Montana History*. Columbia Falls: Huzzah Publishing, 2016.

National Postal Museum. "The History and Experience of African Americans in America's Postal Service," https://postalmuseum.si.edu/AfricanAmericanHistory/p16.html

Shirley, Gayle C. *More than Petticoats: Remarkable Montana Women*. Kearney: Morris Book Publishing, 2011.

Albright, Syd, "A Legend in Her Own Time: Stagecoach Mary," *Post Falls Press*, February 7, 2016.

Radeska, Tijana. "Mary Fields—The First African-American Woman Employed as a Mail Carrier in the United States." *The Vintage News*, October 10, 2010. https://www.thevintagenews.com/2016/10/10/mary-fields-first-african-american-woman-employed-mail-carrier-united-states-2/

Wagner, Tricia Martineau. *African American Women of the Old West*. Helena, MT: Twodot, 2007.

"Women Mail Carriers," USPS, June 2007, https://about.usps.com/who-we-are/postal-history/women-carriers.pdf

Crockett, Zachary. "Mary Fields: Former Slave, Pioneer Woman, Certified Badass," *Priceonomics*, n.d., https://priceonomics.com/mary-fields-former-slave-pioneer-woman-certified/

On the Internet
"Don't Mess with 'Stagecoach Mary' Fields," AllenCity TV (Youtube). https://www.youtube.com/watch?v=khhlwpxrtFk

Enss, Chris. "Wild Women of the West: Stagecoach Mary," *Cowgirl*, August 30, 2017. https://cowgirlmagazine.com/stagecoach-mary/

GLOSSARY

buckskin—A soft, strong type of leather that is made from the skin of a deer or sheep.

chambermaid (CHAYM-ber-mayd)—A person who cleans bedrooms in a hotel, ship, or other type of lodging.

chaplain (CHAP-lin)—A priest or Christian religious leader who performs religious services and counseling for the military, hospitals, and prisons.

convent (KON-vent)—The house or building in which a group of nuns lives.

frontier (fron-TEER)—An area where few people live.

homesteader (HOHM-steh-der)—Someone who claims and farms a piece of land.

Jesuit (JEH-zwit)—A man who is a member of the Roman Catholic Society of Jesus.

literate (LIH-tuh-rit)—Able to read and write.

manicured (MAN-ih-kyoord)—Groomed; well maintained.

mission (MIH-shun)—A place or building where religious work is performed.

outpost (OUT-pohst)—A town that is located far from other towns or cities.

parishioner (puh-RISH-ner)—A person who is a member of a Christian church.

GLOSSARY

Riding a stagecoach was a great way to see the beauty of early America.

pioneer (py-uh-NEER)—Someone who is the first to explore or live in a place. Also, a person who is the first to do something or come up with a new idea.

trapper—Someone who catches wild animals in traps and kills them for their fur.

PHOTO CREDITS: Cover, pp. 1, 5, 6, 7, 8, 10, 11, 13, 15, 16, 17, 20, 21, 22, 23 (background), 25, 26, 29, 30, 31, 33, 34, 35, 36, 39, 41, 47—Public Domain; pp. 2–3—Burke & Atwell, Chicago; p. 9—HauiM2/Pixabay; p. 14—Kimberly Vardeman; p. 19—Aneil Lutchman; p. 23 (buckboard)—Dwight Burdette; p. 27—Tomfriedel; p. 28—SMU Central University Libraries; p. 37—Billy Hathorn; p. 38—Montana.gov. Every measure has been taken to find all copyright holders of material used in this book. In the event any mistakes or omissions have happened within, attempts to correct them will be made in future editions of the book.

47

INDEX

Blackfeet   17, 22
Black Robes   21
Brondel, Bishop   34
Buck, Horace   23
Buck, James   23
Buck (Mary's father)   12
Buckskin dresses   28
Cooper, Gary   38
Curry, John W.   11
Dunne, Edmond   14, 15
Dunne, Sarah Amadeus   9, 14, 15, 17, 18, 20, 22, 30, 32, 35
Fields, Mary (Stagecoach Mary)
   birthday   12, 29, 38
   clothing   15, 28, 35
   death   38
   as mail carrier   4, 6–10, 35–38
   in Montana   6, 18, 20–22, 24, 25, 26–28, 29, 30, 32, 34–38
   laundry service   37
   restaurants   35
   skills   12, 16, 24, 25, 26, 27, 35–37
   temper   14, 16, 30, 32, 33, 34
Hickok, Wild Bill   31
Holliday, Doc   31
Jesuit priests   18
Johnson, Andrew   13
Johnson, Dolly   13
Landesmith, Eli   26

McBride, Sister   34
Martin, Polly   39
Mary of the Angels, Sister   20
Minnetonka   20
Moses (Mary's mule)   4, 6, 7, 8, 37
Natchez (steamboat)   14–15
National Association of Letter Carriers   11
National Postal Museum   37
Northern Pacific Railroad   20
Robert E. Lee (steamboat)   14–15
Saint Ignatius, Sister   22
St. Peter's Mission   10, 16, 17, 18, 20, 21, 22, 29, 30, 32, 35, 38
Saint Thomas, Sister   22
saloons   31, 34, 38
slavery   12, 13, 14, 30
Stanislaus, Mother   20
Susanna (Mary's mother)   12
Ursuline Convent and Girls School   16, 17
Ursuline Convent of the Sacred Heart   15
wagons   4–10, 21, 28, 32
   buckboard   20, 23, 24, 26
   farm   24
   freight   5
   mail   36, 37, 39
White Crow   22
wolves   7–9